Lighthouses of England

WOLF ROCK

by

Martin Boyle

B&T Publications

PUBLISHED BY B&T PUBLICATIONS
10 Orchard Way · Highfield · Southampton
Hampshire SO17 1RD

Copyright © 1997, Martin Boyle
who is the recognised author of this work
in accordance with Section 77 of the Copyright,
Design and Patents Act 1988.

All rights reserved. No part of this publication
may be reproduced or transmitted in any form
or by any means, electronic or mechanical;
photocopying, recording, or any storage and
retrieval system, without the permission of the
copyright holder.

International Standard Book Number

ISBN 1-901043-07-X

International Standard Serial Number

ISSN 1363 8009

Typesetting by SPITZER · COMPUTERGRAFIK

Lighthouses of Southwest England
(Cornwall and Isles of Scilly)

1. Trevose Head
2. Godrevy Island
3. Pendeen
4. Longships
5. Round Island
6. Bishop Rock

7. St. Agnes Island (discontinued)
8. Peninnis
9. Wolf Rock
10. Tater–du
11. Lizard Point
12. St. Anthony's

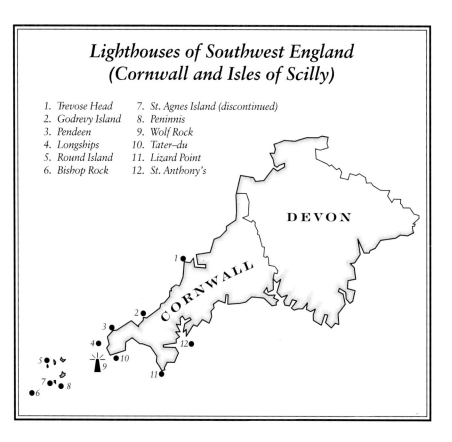

SPECIAL ACKNOWLEDGEMENT

The author gratefully acknowledges the invaluable help of the Corporation of Trinity House, its Publication Officer and Media Director, its Director of Engineering and his exceptional Staff, with the full co-operation of the Master and Elder Brethren.

3

Contents

Reproduced with kind permission of Trinity House

WOLF ROCK

POSITION: 49°56'07" N - 05°48'02" W
LOCATION: Between Isles of Scilly and Cornwall
NO. ON ADMIRALTY LIST OF LIGHTS: 0030
PRESENT TOWER BUILD: 1862–1869
DESIGNER & RESIDENT ENGINEER: James Walker–James Nicholas Douglass
COMPOSITION OF STRUCTURE: Circular granite
HEIGHT OF TOWER - FOUNDATION TO GALLERY: 115ft 11ins (35.33m)
FOCAL PLANE OF LIGHT: 110ft (33.53m) AHWST*
LIGHT FIRST LIT: 1st January 1870
AUTOMATED: July 1988
MONARCH AT TIME OF CONSTRUCTION: Queen Victoria (1837–1901)
*AHWST = Above High Water Spring Tide, Old Terminology

WOLF ROCK LIGHTHOUSE

Graveyard of Ships

Barely visible from Land's End, facing the full fury of the Atlantic Ocean, stands the lonely granite tower on the Wolf Rock. In terms of bleak and isolated locations, there is only one other lighthouse near the Isles of Scilly more exposed, and that is Bishop Rock.

The Wolf marks one point in an important triangle of maritime navigational references, making this dangerous area one of the best lit waterways in the British Isles. It is eight miles from the Longships light, and 23 miles from Lizard Point.

Before the Wolf Rock was lit, it was barely visible during normal tides and submerged to about 5ft (1.52m) at high spring water level. At low tide it stands a rugged 17ft (5.18m) above sea level, which makes it a treacherous obstacle for shipping, especially during the night. The depth of water around this lonely rock is about 34 fathoms (204ft - 62.18m), which has become the graveyard of numerous mariners and their ships.

Cornish Wreckers – Cavern Blocked

The name '*Wolf*' is believed to have derived from the noise that was produced, when air compressed by the sea, was forced through a fissure in a cavern below the Rock surface. It has been said that during the early 16th century, Cornish wreckers filled this cavern with large rocks. They believed the noise was preventing ships from being wrecked, which in turn deprived them of their winter incomes from salvage. Apparently the law was on their side, which was based on '*Custom and Descent*'.

What Do We Call The Rock ?

During the 13th & 14th centuries priests around Cornwall and the Isles of Scilly recorded on their early rutters (sailing directions) the name '*Yulf*' or '*Wulf*'. However, the first officially recognised sea chart produced by the Dutch in their '*Sea Mirrour*', drawn up in Amsterdam in 1658, shows the Rock as '*Wolf*'. In '*De Witts Atlas*' of 1688, the name was shown as '*The Gulfe*'. Further confusion followed four years later, when a French sea chart '*Le Neptune Francaise*' called it '*Le Loup*'. Yet within twelve months the same chart maker, under the heading '*English Channel*', called the Rock '*Le Housen de Wolf*'. [1]

In 1701 Edmund Nalley, on his sea chart '*English Channel*', provided the first British reference to the Rock and named it '*Gulf*'. For nearly 59 years users of the English Channel appeared to have agreed, because most sea charts referred to the Rock as '*Gulf*' or '*Gulf Wolf*'. During this period successive chart makers such as Johannes van Kenlen (Amsterdam), Borlase, whose '*Islands of Scilly*' were published by Grenville Collins (England) and the '*Neptune L'An VI de la République*' (Paris) all agreed on the '*Gulf Wolf*'. Yet in 1776 the '*Neptune Mers du Nord*' of Paris, drawn up by the Depôt de la Marine, recorded the Rock as '*Gulf Roche*'.

Between 1798 and 1802 the *'Neptune'* referred to the *'Wolf Rock'* or *'Le Loup'*. But then, in 1825, it appears to agree with all the other chart makers, that the official name should be *'Wolf Rock'*. This was shown on its chart for Land's End, *'Des Sorlinges'*, produced by the Depôt General de la Marine and signed by a Lieutenant Mackenzie. From this time the name has been known as *'Wolf Rock'*. [1]

A Bell Buoy

The first recorded proposal to Trinity House, for a means to mark the Wolf Rock, was made in 1750. A group of concerned shipowners suggested that a large buoy with a bell could be sited near to the Rock. However, when knowledge of these proposals reached the local Cornish fishermen, they strongly objected. These men felt that the so called *'musick'* would frighten the fish away. There were also threats, that any buoy located by the Wolf Rock would be destroyed by the local wrecking communities.

Lieutenant Henry Smith

A formal attempt at highlighting the dangerous Wolf Rock, was implemented by Lieutenant Henry Smith in 1791. But prior to petitioning Trinity House, he discussed a project with a Cornish miner Thomas Curtis. The idea put forward by this miner, was to blow up the Rock. This was not as silly as it seems, because Thomas Curtis is accredited as being the person who had achieved a method of placing explosives under water prior to detonation. He had already provided proof for his system, with a project successfully completed in the submarine Wherry Mine near Penzance. But Lt. Smith realised that blowing up the Wolf Rock would not bring profit, in fact it was far too expensive. He believed that it would be more financially rewarding to erect a beacon on the Rock and to levy shipping for its use. [2]

Trinity House considered the proposals from Lt. Smith and obtained a Letters Patent for the Wolf Rock. At the same time the Corporation was issued with another Patent for the Longships, with the intention of erecting a lighthouse. These documents were warranted in February 1795. In the usual practise for the Corporation during this period, the Lieutenant was granted a 50 year lease and the right to collect a levy from shipping. He was expected to take on both projects, a beacon on the Wolf Rock and a lighthouse on the Longships. Although Lt. Smith made several attempts at erecting a beacon on the Wolf Rock, they were all washed away by the sea within weeks of being sited. Within 18 months, he had bordered on bankruptcy and surrendered his lease to Trinity House. [3]

A Bronze Wolf

Following the failed attempts by Lt. Smith, a strange idea was put into operation for the Wolf Rock. A wolf was cast out of bronze and designed to howl when the wind blew through it. After casting it was taken out to the Rock, but the hazardous sea and weather conditions prevented its installation. The men involved with this venture, spent four very dangerous days in atrocious conditions, waiting nearby to complete the project. As the weather got worse, the attempt was abandoned. Although recorded in the Papers of the Institution of Civil Engineers, no-one has admitted designing or financing this project. Surely this idea must constitute some claim to fame. [1]

Granite Masonry Tower – Robert Stevenson

It was not until 1823 when the Admiralty contacted Trinity House with regards to siting a lighthouse on Wolf Rock. These discussions followed the involvement of Robert Stevenson, the Engineer-in-Chief of the Northern Lighthouse Board. He had designed a granite tower which he estimated would take 15 years to build at a cost of £150,000. The Elder Brethren of Trinity House rejected the proposals solely on the basis of cost. They also felt that such a design would be too rigid for the location and not realistically possible.

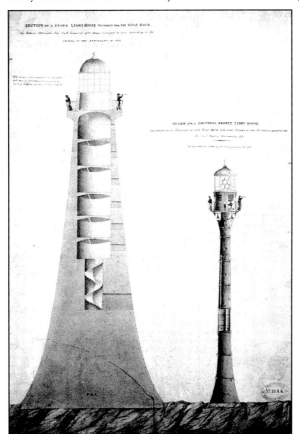

Around the same time as Robert Stevenson put forward his Wolf designs, another much respected engineer for the Admiralty, Commander Samuel Browne R.N., proposed the construction of a lighthouse made out of cast bronze. It was to be manufactured in a kit form, then erected to the same height as the existing Eddystone tower. The estimated cost for this project would be £16,000, with the contract completed in six month.

Although formal consideration was given to the proposed bronze lighthouse, the memories of the difficulties encountered with the former beacons, and the

Drawing reproduced with kind permission of Trinity House

8

tremendous power of the surrounding seas, it was not felt to be a suitable option. Yet it is interesting to notice the details, included on the Trinity Archive drawing by Commander Browne. It showed four keepers, apparently enjoying a carefree life on the new tower. One of them was drawn leaning against the gallery hand-rail, another stood looking through a telescope, with the third keeper reading a newspaper whilst relaxing in a sea-side deck chair. The last keeper was shown standing inside of what appears to be a strange looking bedroom, with grand style curtains covering the windows.

Wolf Rock Beacons – James Walker

A further thirteen years passed, and with the dramatic rise in sea trade so came the tragic increase in ships being lost around the Wolf Rock. This prompted the Elder Brethren of Trinity House to instruct their consultant engineer, James Walker, to design and establish a beacon on the Rock. Between 1836–40 this project was given to John Thurburn, an experienced engineer associated with the Walker & Burges practice in Great George Street, London.

To erect the first Wolf beacon, designed by James Walker, John Thurburn noted in his diary, that considering the atrocious working conditions the builders had to endure, it was a remarkable achievement. The base of this beacon consisted of a cast- iron cone, 18ft (5.49m) in diameter and 24ft (7.32m) high. Set in the centre of the top of the cone was a 1ft (305mm) diameter oak mast, that protruded 6ft (1.83m) above the structure. This 12ft (3.6m) long mast was set into a brass shoe-

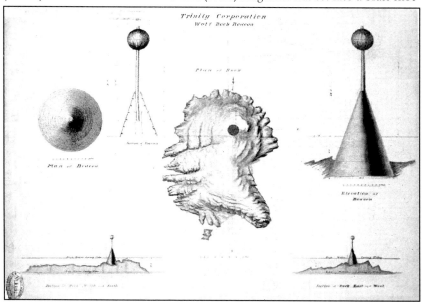

Drawing reproduced with kind permission of Trinity House

9

type cylinder inside of the cone, with the remaining space filled with granite rubble and strong marine cement. The weight of the cone section was between 118 to 220 tons and it was anchored to the Wolf Rock with 4inch (102mm) thick iron bolts with wedged ends. Holes were bored into the rock surface with inverted cone sections, into which the split and wedged bolts were driven. A mix of molten lead and pewter was then poured around the bolts. Each of the twenty holes were sunk to a depth of 18 inches (457mm). Fixed to the oak mast was a 4ft (1.22m) diameter copper globe, with its centre set at 28ft (8.53m) AHWST. The project took 302½ hours over a period of 4 years to complete. The final accounts for the work came to £11,298. However within six weeks of completion, a severe storm, in November 1840, snapped off the mast and washed it away. [1]

For two years nothing was done to replace the broken mast, as Trinity House believed that the white painted base would be sufficient. In fact it was clearly noted on various rutters and Admiralty charts. During the summer of 1842 Nicholas Douglass, the father of the Douglass family of engineers, was appointed by James Walker to erect another mast. This time it was made out of wrought iron, nearly 9 inches (229mm) in diameter, and set into a cast-iron cylinder lining. A 5ft (1.52m) diameter brass ball was fitted to the top of the mast. It was believed that this hollow ball would be more easily spotted. During the winter months of 1842–43 a severe storm crashed on to the beacon and bent the mast nearly 3ft (914mm) out of upright. When a survey was carried out the following summer, it was considered not to be a problem. However another storm in February 1844 snapped the iron mast and swept it into the sea. [1]

Once more the Wolf Rock beacon stood only as a cast-iron cone, until Nicholas Douglass and his workforce were sent back to fit another mast. By July 1845 the work had been completed, this time including the fitting of cast iron stays. A new ball, which allowed the water to pass through, was installed. For the next two years the Wolf Rock beacon remained intact, but during a hurricane force gale in March 1848 the mast was washed away like all its predecessors, and this time even the base cone loosened from its foundations. [1]

Last Beacon on Wolf Rock

The last beacon on the Wolf Rock was erected in August 1850. Now the mast was 1ft (305mm) in diameter, with a 3ft (914mm) brass ball fitted to the top of the 12ft (3.66m) high pole. The belief was that the ball had been sited too close to the cone and with a longer mast, much of the sea's power would have been lost. This structure remained intact until it was taken down during the construction of the lighthouse.

In his report to the Institution of civil Engineers around 1870, James Nicholas Douglass stated that the number of ships being wrecked on the Wolf Rock had been significantly reduced since the introduction of the beacons. He also commented that the only cost of its upkeep for the past 19 years, had been for groups of painters applying fresh coats of red lead and white paint. Yet there are other records in the Lloyd's Register, which state, that although the beacon gave good service during daylight hours, it was barely visible at night or in bad weather, and so it provided little or no warning to shipping, often with disastrous results. [1]

A Mariner's Nightmare – Shipwrecks

An insight to the dangers posed by the Wolf Rock can be provided from Lloyd's Register, now preserved in the Guildhall Library, London. On the 9th January 1855, the French sloop RAILLUER was enroute from Bordeaux to Bristol. Her Master, Captain Roi, was an experienced seaman and familiar with this route from France to England. But as night fell, the RAILLUER struck the Wolf Rock. Captain Roi, and his crew of seven, had only minutes to launch the longboat before the merchant ship sank. After drifting for nearly two days, they were finally rescued by the Revenue cutter BADGER near Penzance. [4]

One of the most worrying nightmares for the Victorian mariner was fog. On one such night, the 11th May 1856, the Cornish brig MENTOR left Devoran in Cornwall, bound for Swansea with a cargo of copper. As the fog got thicker, her Master, Captain William Pearce, lost his bearings and ran into the Wolf Rock. Before the crew could take to their boat, a huge wave lifted the MENTOR off the Rock. Although his ship was taking on water, Captain Pearce believed he could get her back to the mainland. Within three hours the water was coming into the ship faster than the crew could pump it out. By this time the Truro sloop GEORGE had come to the MENTOR's assistance. But within ten minutes of her arrival the order was given to abandon ship. As the last of her crew was taken on board the GEORGE, the MENTOR sank. [4]

Problems with heavy rain and fog are one thing, but add the difficulties of language, and it will makes matters worse. At 02.30 hours on the 16th March 1861, the lookout on the Prussian barque ASTREA spotted the Wolf Rock. Before her helmsman could take avoiding action, she ran into the steepest part of the Rock. As one of the longboats was lowered, a huge wave crashed down onto it and swept everyone away. Another boat was lowered, but before other members of the crew could join the lone seaman in it, a wave washed it from the side of the ship. Of the two remaining longboats on board the ASTREA, another was smashed by the sea in its davits, and the last one dropped bow first and sank like a stone.

As the ASTREA lurched fiercely to one side, her Captain was seriously injured when a water cask fell on him. With the barque settling deeper into the water, the remaining ten crewmen dragged their Captain into the foretop. For nearly two and half hours, the ASTREA remained afloat, but with her stern section awash. At this time the Newlyn lugger TRIUMPH arrived on the scene, but the rough sea prevented her from approaching close enough to rescue the stricken crewmen. Above the tremendous roar of the sea, the Captain of the TRIUMPH tried to talk with the Prussian crew. He told them to lower their boats and he would pick them up. Other members of the TRIUMPH's crew tried to make the crewmen understand that they did not have any boats of their own to send over. In turn the Prussian crew attempted to explain that all of their longboats were gone. Suddenly, during this confusing time, a huge wave overshot the Wolf Rock forcing the

ASTREA clear. Within minutes she sank stern first. Of those who had originally survived, the Captain and one young Prussian were the only two to be rescued. [4]

Once more the fog came in, and now even thicker than before. As the TRIUMPH made her way towards Penzance, an unknown schooner collided with her and snapped off the mizzen mast. During the following afternoon, as the helpless seaman in the only surviving longboat of the ASTREA drifted towards Land's End and the dangerous Longships reef, he was spotted and rescued by the Newlyn lugger BAND OF HOPE. [4]

Lighthouse Designed By James Walker

Prior to the events of the ASTREA, around the beginning of 1860, the Elder Brethren of Trinity House had instructed James Walker to prepare the plans, designs and estimates for constructing a lighthouse on the Wolf Rock. His detailed drawings showed that it was intended for the proposed granite tower to be built as part of the Rock and not just stand upon it. The project was sanctioned by the Board of Trade in November 1861. James Nicholas Douglass was appointed by James Walker to be the resident engineer. The contract would start as soon as he had completed the building of the Smalls lighthouse off the Welsh coast.

James Walker
Reproduced with kind permission of Trinity House

On completion of the Smalls contract, James Douglass re-employed many of the construction workers and took them to Penzance. The vessel used during the Smalls project was a 60 ton tug, which James Douglass hired for use at the Wolf Rock. When the tug left Wales, it carried most of the workforce, with all of the equipment used during the Smalls contract towed behind in five barges. Each of these barges was fitted with rails and roller carriages, which allowed easy movement of the heavy granite blocks. The total weight each of the barges could carry, was just over 40 tons. [5]

Shore base at Penzance

Before work began on the Wolf Rock in 1862, Trinity House constructed a pur-pose-built shore base and workshops. All the granite stones for the lighthouse were prepared to specially calculated templates before being transported to site. Today this shore base is home to the Trinity House National Lighthouse Centre. A long jetty was also built close to the shore base, to accommodate a purpose-built 100 ton schooner. This ship was used to provide quarters for the workforce, and on completion of the contract, it became one of the Tenders for Trinity House.

On the 1st July 1861 James Douglass went to the Wolf Rock to carry out a full survey. He was warned by the Master of the Trinity Tender several times about the unpredictable nature of the sea. Although the water washed over the surface of the Rock, he continued with his survey until the sea almost swept him away. Within half an hour of this event, the weather had dramatically changed, with waves overshooting the Wolf Rock. James Douglass soon realised that he had overstayed his visit, but when he signalled for a longboat to collect him, 4ft (1.22m) swells threatened to smash it against the Rock. The Master of the Trinity Tender ordered a rope to be thrown to James Douglass, and in a very ungentlemanly fashion he was then hauled through the sea to the longboat. [5]

James Nicholas Douglass
Reproduced with kind permission of Trinity House

Between the 17th March and the 29th September 1862, the back-breaking task of preparing the foundations out of the Wolf Rock began. A lookout was positioned on the highest point of the Rock, to warn the workforce about any waves that were likely to overshoot the site. When this occurred, the men grabbed hold of safety ropes and each other until the sea had subsided. Tools, some weighing up to 20 pounds (9.07kg), were regularly washed away. [6]

Sudden Death of James Walker

While the rock surface was being prepared a landing stage was started and much of the foundation pit for the lighthouse blasted and formed. Unfortunately not everything was going as planned. A month after the schooner brought the Wolf Rock workforce back to Penzance, James Walker suffered a heart attack and died. This exceptional civil engineer had seen the project started, but he would never see the Wolf Rock lit.

Following this sad occasion, Trinity House offered James Douglass the position of its first Engineer-in-Chief, which he accepted. At a meeting of the Institution of Civil Engineers in 1863, James Douglass spoke highly of James Walker. He said: *'he led a very rewarding and fruitful life. Although still actively employed at the age of 81, he could see no reason to retire'*. [5]

William Douglass Takes Over From Brother James

As Engineer-in-Chief, it was now impossible for James Douglass to continue as the resident engineer for the Wolf Rock contract. The Elder Brethren decided to appoint his brother William Douglass for this position, which he accepted following the successful completion of the Hanois lighthouse in the Channel Islands. Michael Beazeley was appointed the assistant engineer, who would be responsible for ensuring the granite was dressed properly at the Penzance shore base. [1]

Lead by Example – William Douglass

One of the interesting things to be noted about the various engineers who were in charge of lighthouse construction during the Victorian era, was their *'hands on'* approach to the workforce. This was especially the case with the Douglass family, who

felt it was important to lead by example, rather than by designation. William Douglass clearly felt, that respect had to be worked for, and this became apparent on the numerous times he put the lives of his men before his own. One of these men, William Williams, wrote to the biographer of William Douglass and informed him about his former employer. He wrote: *'Mr. Douglass was always the first to land on the Rock and the last to leave'*. William Williams also commented on the occasions when the support boat was unable to come close to the Wolf Rock, to take the workforce off. He stated: *'and when necessary for the workmen to be hauled through the surf "the Good Master", invariably saw that the line was securely fastened round the waist of each man, before following the last man'*. [6]

William Douglass
Reproduced with kind permission of the Commissioners of Irish Lights

There were also other occasions when the sea washed a worker off the Rock, and with many of them surprisingly unable to swim, William Douglass was always one of the first to dive into the sea to effect a rescue. [6]

On one particular occasion, when some of the workforce were staying in the partly completed lighthouse, the relief tug was unable to make a landing to supply them with much needed provisions. William Douglass asked for volunteers to go with him in a longboat to get the supplies to the stranded men. The Master of the support tug strongly advised him against such action, but William Douglass and four men rowed towards the Rock. William Williams was one of the volunteers and wrote: *'he steered right into the midst of the seething caldron, and with infinite coolness and skill manoeuvred her there – though she was in momentary danger of being swamped'*. William Williams also stated, that the actions of *"the Good Master"* resulted in a rope being thrown to the men on the landing stage. Supplies were then loaded into an oil drum, which the workers pulled through the surf to the Rock. [6]

Building Details – Working Seasons

The second working season for the Wolf Rock contract began on the 20th February 1863. During this period, up to the 24th October, Michael Beazeley organised his workforce with the preparation of the granite masonry up to the sixth course. Each of these blocks of stone weighed between 2 and 3 tons and they were fitted together to check they matched the templates. As soon as they had been assembled, Michael Beazeley numbered them ready for taking to site.

This season also saw remarkable progress with the preparation of the foundation pit on the Wolf Rock. Not only was the blasting expertly carried out by the Cornish miners, but the stone cutters from Wales carved the rough area to receive the double dovetailed first course of masonry. This

Walker beacon on Wolf Rock landing platform. Reproduced with kind permission of Trinity House

work was stated as being to between plus or minus ¼ inch (6mm) of the required tolerance. Near the end of the season the foundation base was completed with much of the massive landing stage ahead of schedule. [1]

The third year of the Wolf Rock contract began on the 9th April 1864 and would continue until the 5th November. During the afternoon of the 6th August, William Douglass brought Michael Beazeley out to the Rock, to have the honour of setting the first granite block into position. This particular stone weighed 3 tons. By the end of this working season a total of 37 stones were set into position and pegged for extra stability with gunmetal spikes.

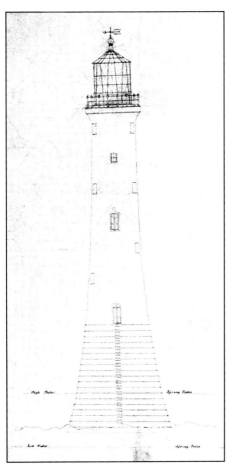

Line drawing of Wolf Rock lighthouse.
Kind permission of Trinity House

The actual operation to move each granite block was well rehearsed, from procedures learnt during the construction of the Smalls tower. William Douglass left most of this part of the contract to the men, who had originally been employed at the previous lighthouse. Firstly the granite blocks were loaded on to the small trucks in the barges at Penzance. On arrival at the Wolf Rock the barge would be tied up to the landing stage. From here each stone would be hauled by a chain to the stern section of the barge. The iron derrick crane, set up on the landing stage, then raised the stone clear of the barge. Allowances were always made for the swell of the sea, before the crane swung the block of granite to its required position. William Douglass commented to his brother James, that the men were so experienced with this offloading that they were able to lift the granite blocks safely on to the Rock, even though there was a 12ft (3.6m) swell. [1]

The winter months of 1864–65 proved to be horrendous. It was feared that all the hard work on the Wolf Rock would be ruined. Storms and gales continued through March, until on the 11th April, William Douglass decided the project could continue. On arrival to the Wolf Rock, none of the granite blocks were missing or even loose. Only part of the derrick on the landing stage had been washed away.

As 1865 progressed, William Douglass decided to extend the working season up to the 17th December. During this time, 41 landings were made on the Rock by the workforce, with a total of just 250 hours actual working time. When the season finished, the lighthouse was constructed up to the fourth course of stones with 34 granite blocks of the fifth set into position. But on the 24th November, a tremendous storm raged around the Wolf Rock. Trees were uprooted on the Isles of Scilly and numerous vessels, which ran for the safety of a harbour along the Cornish coast, were driven ashore before they could reach their destinations.

Two days after the storm had abated, William Douglass took his workforce back to the Wolf Rock and found that all 34 stones of the fifth course had been swept away. At first he noted in his diary that he believed the design strength of the lighthouse was now in doubt. However further investigations revealed that his worries were unfounded. During the storm the 1,544 ton ship STAR OF ENGLAND had narrowly missed the Wolf Rock. Her Captain had ordered the mizzenmast to be cut down to reduce the vessel's top weight. As the mast was felled it swept across the Rock, ripping the heavy granite blocks off the partly built tower and leaving deep gouges from its chains across the workings. [3]

Back at the Penzance shorebase Michael Beazeley was having a better season with all the granite blocks prepared for building the Wolf Rock lighthouse up to the 18th course of masonry. Apart from the loss of the 34 stones, William Douglass felt that 1865 had been a good year. [1]

When the workforce returned to the Rock on the 5th March 1866, William Douglass had already been on the site for two days. He had carried out a full survey of the workings, prior to the contract continuing. From this date until the 13th October, the 9th course of granite blocks and 10 stones of the 10th course were set into position.

During this season a telescopic crane was erected. When the work finished for the year, it was securely anchored at 23ft (7m) above the high water mark. Over the following winter months, severe gales and storms brought mountainous waves crashing down onto the site. The tremendous force of the sea snapped the 16in (406mm) diameter by 1¼in (36mm) thick tubular shaft, flush to the top of the partly built tower.

Back in Penzance, this season had allowed the workforce of Michael Beazeley to complete the dressing of all the stones required, up to the 26th course. William Douglass commented to his brother, that the atmosphere and attitude of everyone at the shorebase was *'commendable'*. [1]

Heavy storms and gales continued to pound the Isles of Scilly and the south coast of Cornwall until after Easter. During this time several ships had come to grief on many of the rugged Cornish beaches and rocks. This raging weather effectively delayed the Wolf Rock contract until the 6th May.

On their arrival at the Wolf Rock, the first priority of the workforce was to replace the broken shaft of the crane. This also meant obtaining a new upper section which had been washed away. Shortly after this repair had been carried out, the weather conditions changed in favour of the contract. By the end of the season the lighthouse had been built to the 23rd course of masonry, with 8 stones of the 24th also set in position, while at the Penzance depot, all the granite blocks up to the 39th course had been prepared, and were numbered ready for shipment.

On the 13th June the summer period was exceptionally calm, which prompted the foreman mason to ask William Douglass if the men could remain on the Rock.

He felt that the contract would be speeded up if the men could start earlier in the morning and not have the delay of getting from the schooner to the Rock. Permission was granted, which made it the first recorded time that anyone had stayed overnight on the Wolf Rock. [1]

This was the 7th year of the Wolf Rock contract, with its working season start-

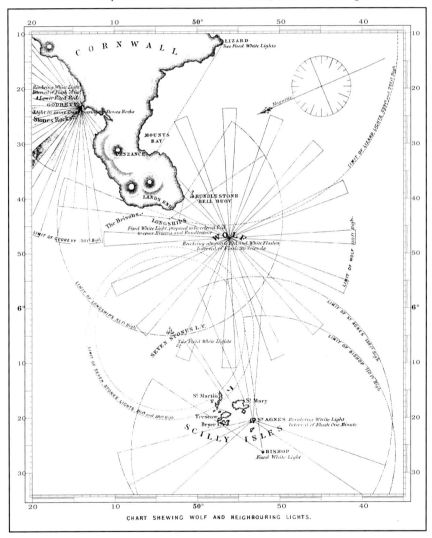

CHART SHEWING WOLF AND NEIGHBOURING LIGHTS.

Chart of Wolf Rock and neighbouring lights
Reproduced with kind permission of Trinity House

ing on the 31st March. On the 17th and 18th June, William Douglass assisted with the erection of a steam winch, that was sited on top of the partly completed tower. This winch had its own boilers, which powered a pair of 8in (200mm) cylinders, each with a 12in (305mm) stroke. When it was first connected to the cables of the crane on the 29th June, the lifting time for the granite blocks was reduced to 2½ minutes. Prior to this, it normally took the strength of ten men and 15 minutes to raise these stones, using the crane and its former block and tackle.

This method of lifting the granite and other heavy items with a steam winch, was considered to be the first time it had been applied for use on a tidal rock. From the day it was brought into operation, until it was dismantled, the winch remained in faithful service without any major problems. [1]

On the 16th March, the Douglass workforce began the last year of the Wolf Rock contract. Many of the men were able to stay in the partly completed tower, instead of returning each night to the schooner. This resulted in the construction programme rapidly progressing. By the early part of July, William Douglass was able to inform Trinity House that the last stage of the gallery was near completion. On the 19th of this month a committee of Elder Brethren arrived on site, with the Deputy Master, Sir Frederick Arrow, officiating with the setting of the last block of granite.

Following this event, which occurred about 14.00 hours, an informal 'topping out ceremony' was provided on board the support schooner. In the traditional

Wolf Rock lighthouse around 1955. With kind permission of Trinity House

way of these times, *'much wine and ale was consumed, and the men well pleased'*. It can only be assumed that a final comment by Sir Frederick Arrow on *'much merriment'* meant, the workforce did not return to the Wolf Rock after the celebration. [6]

An Impressive Feat of Engineering – Landing Stage

During the first four years of the Wolf Rock contract, half of the Douglass workforce were employed in constructing a massive landing stage. Much has been written about the actual lighthouse, yet surprisingly not much about the harsh, and often life-threatening conditions, endured by the Cornish masons on the landing stage. On numerous occasions the men were washed off the Rock and into the sea. Some of them broke limbs, with others suffering from deep lacerations and serious bruising. Yet with all these difficulties, no one actually died from their injuries.

Part of the landing stage workforce were initially employed at the Penzance depot, where they prepared all the pick-dressed granite masonry. Nearly 15,000 blocks of granite 2ft (609mm) x 1ft (305mm) x 6ins (152mm); each weighing about 1½ cwt (76.2kg), were required for the landing stage. Other larger pieces were also used for the steps and coping stones. All of this Ashlar granite masonry was set into position using English Bond, with a composite mix of 1 to 1 granite sand and Medina Roman cement.

In total, the landing stage was a massive 14,564 cu.ft. (412m³) of masonry, that weighed approximately 1079 tons (1093 tonnes). [1]

Wolf Rock Beacon on landing stage, THV STELLA. With kind permission of Gerry Douglas-Sherwood

During the years that followed the erection of the Wolf Rock lighthouse, this landing stage became a vital inclusion. Without it, relieving the keepers or landing supplies and provisions would have been virtually impossible. [1]

Fog Warning

One of the last items to be installed on the Wolf Rock lighthouse was a 7 cwt (356kg) brass fog bell. It was sited on the gallery with its hammer operated by cables, powered by a Wilkins & Son clockwork mechanism. When originally in service, it sounded 3 times in quick succession every 15 seconds.

The audible range for this bell was recorded as 4 nautical miles, yet this figure seems somewhat doubtful. The distance stated could only have been achieved, when sounded with the wind. In the opposite direction it is more likely that its value was about a quarter of a mile. [1]

Specifications of the Wolf Rock Lighthouse

As a monument to James Walker and all the people involved with its construction, the Wolf Rock lighthouse stands a majestic 115ft (35.33m) in height, from its foundation rock to its gallery. At base level it is 41ft 8ins (12.68m) in diameter. The base is solid to a height of 39ft 5ins (11.98m), except for the area formed in the granite for the freshwater tank. This base was erected in 20 courses of stepped granite blocks, which effectively breaks up the tremendous force of the sea. It also greatly helps in the prevention of the sea funnelling upwards and overshooting the lantern during severe storms or gales. From the base rock to the 19th course of masonry, numerous gun-metal bolts 2ins (50mm) in diameter and 1ft (305mm) long were used, which penetrated 9ins (225mm) into the block of granite below.

At the 20th course of granite the entrance doorway was formed. The walls at this level were 7ft 9ins (2.36m) thick, and from here, they tapered externally to 2ft 3ins (686mm), to the course of stones below the cornice of the gallery.

Up to the 7th course of masonry, at the level of the highest spring water tides, all the granite blocks were double dovetailed and set into position using Medina Roman Cement. This cement was mostly supplied by the Government Stores in Chatham, although some deliveries of this quick drying marine composite came from Francis & Co., who also provided the Portland cement for the remainder of the tower.

In a similar fashion as the base, all the remaining courses of granite for the lighthouse were also double dovetailed. For strength and hardness, similar to the Ashlar granite, a mixture of 1 to 1 composite mortar; employing granite sand from the Balleswidden tin mines near Penzance, was used to set each course of masonry.

The centre point of gravity for the building is 36ft 3ins (11.05m) above the solid base foundation. In total the completed tower contains 44,506cu.ft (1.246m³) of granite and weighs approximately 3297 tons (3350 tonnes). [1]

Granite Floor Biscuits - Telescopic Crane

One important design feature of the Wolf Rock lighthouse was the method utilised to form the central portion of the floor slabs. Using the same principle as carried out in the Smalls lighthouse, a circular slab of granite was rebated to form a 'stone biscuit'.

This system of construction was to allow a stable and stormproof means for erecting a telescopic crane. Extensible circular bracing rings around the centralised 16in (406mm) diameter by 1¼in (36mm) thick tubular iron crane, fitted snugly against oak blocks, placed on the surface of the internal walls of the tower. In lengths of about 10ft (3.05m), this shaft was increased in height by further sections of tubing, with the joints held securely with large cotter pins.

As each floor level was reached, cantilevered slabs of dressed granite were set into position around the crane. After a few more courses of masonry had been built on top, the crane lifted the granite biscuits, which were then leaned against the internal walls of the tower.

This method of working continued until the gallery level was completed, at which time another crane was erected on top of the tower. When the telescopic crane was dismantled in its various sections, the granite biscuits were lowered into their central positions. [1]

Inside the Wolf Rock Lighthouse

James Walker designed the interior of the Wolf Rock tower into seven floor levels with the lantern fixed on top. From the landing stage, access into the tower was through a pair of gun-metal doors, which had a combined weight of nearly half a ton (508kg). On entering the lighthouse, each floor level was reached by an open-plan cast-iron geometrical staircase, that wound its way into the lantern room.

Situated beneath the ground floor level was the large granite tank, capable of holding about 900 galls (4081 lts) of fresh drinking water. It was 6ft 6ins (1.98m) deep and 7ft (2.13m) in diameter. Access into the tank was through a gun-metal manhole, set into the granite floor. The dimension of the entrance lobby was 8ft 6ins (2.59m) in diameter and 10ft (3.05m) in height to the centre of its concave ceiling. [1]

This first floor level formed the station's woodshed and coal-store, which was originally used by the keepers for cooking and heating. There were also two large wooden barrels, which contained sawdust or sand. This would be spread on the floor of the oil room in cases of spillage. The dimensions for this coal store were 9ft 6ins (2.89m) in diameter and 9ft (2.74m) in height. [1]

On the second floor was the main provisions store which contained purpose-built curved cupboards, made from English oak. Numerous shelves were also fitted, some of pine, the others of oak. These too were shaped to follow the curvature of the walls.

One area of this room was designated for the storage of large barrels, which contained various citrus fruits *'for the prevention of scurvy'*, salt fish and hard oatmeal biscuits. A large supply of potatoes, onions and flour was kept in these barrels and at one time these items were the staple diet for the keepers. One particular recipe looked like a thick brown glutinous substance, liberally infused with slices of onion. This became known as *'Onion Gravy'*.

An iron girder was built into the walls at ceiling height, for carrying the moveable provisions hoist. The arms of this hoist could be extended, to ensure the stores being lifted were kept clear of the external walls. Two large gun-metal doors fronted this room, which had the dimensions of 10ft (3.05m) in diameter and 9ft (2.74m) in height. [1]

Sited around the perimeter of the third floor, were tall cylindrical oak oil tanks which stood on a timber plinth. The contents of these tanks were capable of allowing the lighthouse to remain operational for up to three months.

Each oil tank was connected to the next by a pipe, with one of them attached to a large hand-pump. The keepers used this unit to build up pressure, which

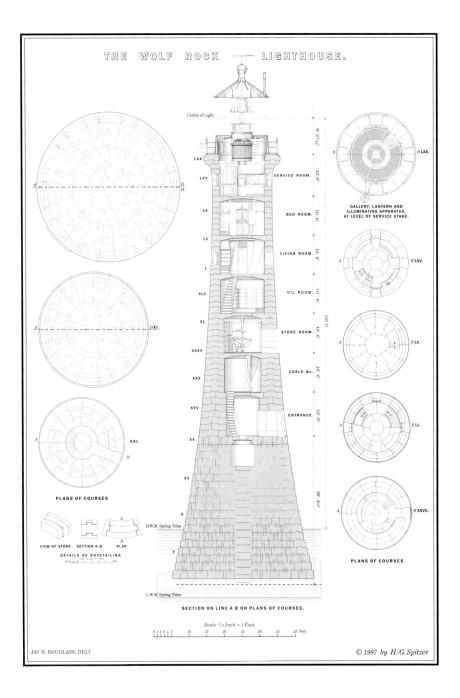

THE WOLF ROCK ⚓ LIGHTHOUSE.

Centre of Light

LXX

LXV — SERVICE ROOM.

LX — BED ROOM.

LV

L — LIVING ROOM.

XLV — OIL ROOM.

XL — STORE ROOM.

XXXV

XXX — COALS &c.

XXV

XX — ENTRANCE.

XV

X — H.W.M. Spring Tides

V

L.W.M. Spring Tides

9' 3"¹¹⁄₁₂"

12' 0"

10' 6"

10' 6"

10' 6"

10' 6"

10' 6"

12' 0"

110 ft

38' 4½"

GALLERY, LANTERN AND ILLUMINATING APPARATUS, AT LEVEL OF SERVICE STAGE.

A — B LXX.

A — B LXV.

A — B LV.

A — B LI.

A — B XXVII.

PLANS OF COURSES

VIEW OF STONE   SECTION A–B   PLAN

DETAILS OF DOVETAILING

PLANS OF COURSES

II.

XI.

XXI.

SECTION ON LINE A B ON PLANS OF COURSES.

Scale: ¹⁄₈ Inch = 1 Foot.

0 1 2 3 4 5   10   15   20   25   30   35   40 Feet.

JAˢ N. DOUGLASS, DELᵀ

© 1997 by H.-G. Spitzer

23

Wolf Rock kitchen during the 1970's.
With kind permission of Gerry Douglas-Sherwood

Banana bunks inside Wolf Rock lighthouse.
With kind permission of Trinity House

forced the oil up, through a small-bore pipeline, into smaller containers in the service room.

To one side of this room were two large ceiling height cupboards, which contained various tools, cleaning utensils and tins of paint for the lighthouse. From this floor level, the dimensions of the rooms above were 11ft (3.35m) in diameter and 9ft (2.74m) in height.

In the fourth floor living room was fitted the specially designed curved cast-iron AGA cooker. Against the opposite wall was positioned the upright cast-iron stove. Flues for both of these units exited through the walls of the lighthouse. Several curved oak dressers and wall cupboards were fitted in every available space. One section was fitted out as a walk-in larder, which was fronted by a large curved floor made out of English oak. [1]

The use of quality English oak was clearly displayed in fifth floor bedroom, with the cabinet-makers skill of the joiners producing exceptional banana-shaped bunks. These splendid units were erected in two tiers, with oak panelled cupboards built under the bottom bunks. Three pairs of these bunks were fitted with tall curved wardrobes between them. Each of the bunks had its own courtesy curtain. These provided privacy in the communal bedroom, and were heavy enough to exclude the daylight. A sideboard style cupboard was also designed to fit under the geometrical staircase. [1]

Apart from the lantern room, the sixth floor area was considered to be the operational heart of the lighthouse. It contained floor to ceiling curved dressers with cupboards underneath. These units held numerous books, a barometer, a clock, charts, weather record pads, the stations log and requisition journal. Other items such as spare wicks, replacement lamps, glass funnels, spare lantern glass, telescope and flags were also kept in this room.

A set of scales and cleaning equipment for the lantern and the lamps etc., were stored in this area. The scales were an important item, because they were used to weigh the oil after each night shift, so a calculation could be made of the previous nights consumption.

Service Room during the 1970's.
With kind permission of Gerry Douglas-Sherwood

There were four windows set into the walls of the lighthouse, each sited at the main points of the compass. When on duty, the keepers only left this room for *'calls of nature'*, to brew up 'make the tea', or to raise a fellow keeper who was due to start his shift.

Apart from the small oil containers in this room, there was also a specially designed ventilation system. Its principle utilised the rising of the hot air generated in the lantern room, it jointly incorporated the vents around the Douglass designed pedestal base. So effective was this system that very little fumes from the paraffin or from the accommodation area were noticeable. [1]

Lantern Room

This particular Douglass designed helical lantern was manufactured by S. Hodge & Sons. Prior to its installation at Wolf Rock, it was taken

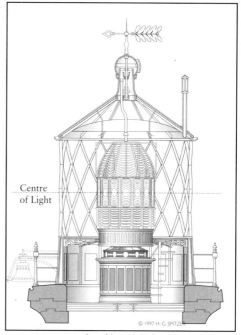

Drawing of Wolf Rock helical lantern
by H.-G. Spitzer

to France and displayed in the Paris Exhibition of 1867. After this time, the majority of the helical designed lanterns were manufactured by Chance Brothers of Smethwick, Birmingham.

The Wolf Rock lantern stood on a 14ft (4.27m) diameter cast-iron pedestal base, 4ft 6ins (1.37m) in height. This base contained numerous hit-and-miss vents, which provided a constant flow of air over the surface of the internal glazing, to prevent the formation of condensation.

An iron grating formed a walkway, which was laid on to ornamental brackets, fitted around the top external perimeter of the pedestal base. This allowed the keepers to have an all round access to the optical apparatus and for cleaning the interior of the lantern.

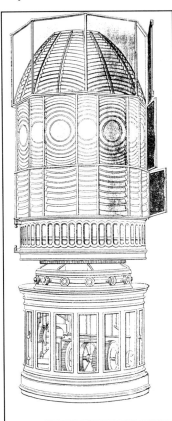

Wolf Rock 1st. order catadioptric apparatus.
With kind permission of Kenneth Sutton-Jones, taken from former drawings by Chance Brothers

The curved glazed area of the lantern was 9ft 6ins (2.86m) in height and constructed with gun-metal window bars. This section was then topped by a 4ft 6in (1.37m) high conical roof, consisting of gun-metal rafters covered with thick copper sheets. In turn this roof was surmounted by a tall ball finial chimney and arrow-shaped weather-vane. [1]

1st Order Optical Apparatus

This optical lens assembly, a 1st. order (920mm focal distance) catadioptric apparatus, was manufactured by Chance Brothers of Birmingham. It was 8ft 6ins (2.58m) in height and 5ft 9ins (1.73in) in diameter. It consisted of 16 panels of refractors and lower prisms, with 8 panels of upper prisms to the main circle of light.

Eight of these panels; with their prisms set at 18°, were provided for the white light, while the other eight panels had their prisms set at 27° and 45°. These directed the light onto a ruby glass panel, which revolved to provide a 30 second flash of bright red.

Prior to fixing these settings, Professor Tyndall, the scientific officer for Trinity House, realised that an arrangement of white and red flashes needed to have a uniform brilliance. He also knew that any light was greatly reduced in its intensity, when shining through a ruby lens.

Experiments were carried out at the Trinity House Lighthouse Depot in Blackwall with distance readings taken from Charlton nearly 2 miles away. From these tests and others, carried out at the Great Ormes Head and Point of Air lighthouses, a ratio of white light was calculated at 21 to 9 which gave a uniform brilliance to both red and white beams. [1]

Wilkins & Son Spring Drive Mechanism

Unlike many other lighthouses established during this period, the original clock-work mechanism for the Wolf Rock equipment was powered by a high tensile spring. Normally the weight factor for a 1st order lens required the more powerful system of a heavy weight descending inside of a hollow cast-iron stanchion. Yet this system seemed quite adequate for this unit. Its only drawback was the need for the spring to be rewound by the keepers after every 4 hours of service. [1]

Assigned Characteristic - Visible Distance

When in operation, the Chance Brothers optic revolved on its roller bearing pedestal base, to provide a red and white flash once every 30 seconds. The recorded visible range for the light was between 14 and 16 nautical miles. The focal plane of the Wolf Rock light is set at 110ft (33.53m) A.H.W.S.T. Its light source was originally provided by an Augustine Fresnel multi-wick capillary lamp. Three years after the station became operational, this was replaced by a more effective multi-wick burner, designed by James Douglass and manufactured by Chance Brothers. [1]

Photo of Wolf Rock, taken around 1919 by Alfred Gibson.
With kind permission of Frank E. Gibson

First Baptism by Storm

Near the completion of the Wolf Rock lighthouse; on the 11th September 1869, the Isles of Scilly and much of the south coast of Cornwall, were hit by near hurricane force gales. Spray from the exceptional waves overshot the lighthouse, which was recorded at about 120ft (36.58m) in height. During this 10 to 11 force westerly gale, the keepers and four construction workers in the tower stated: *'although the shock was distinctly felt with each wave stroke, scarcely any tremor was perceptible'*. [1]

First Lit

On the 1st January 1870, the Trinity House keepers lit the lamp of the Wolf Rock light for the first time. This occasion was witnessed from a distance of about 5 miles by a small committee of Elder Brethren and Michael Beazeley, who were on board a Trinity House vessel. William Douglass was unable to be there for the event, because during the previous month he had handed over the full responsibility of the Wolf Rock contract to Michael Beazeley. The reason for this was, that William Douglass had sailed in a new tug HERCULES to Ceylon (named Sri Lanka since 1972). The purpose for this voyage was to supervise the construction of the Great Basses lighthouse, designed for Trinity House by his brother James. [6]

Final Construction Details

When the figures for the Wolf Rock contract were totalled, Michael Beazeley reported to the Institution of Civil Engineers that *'there had been 8 working seasons, 266 landings on the Rock and 1809½ hours worked, or nearly 181 days of 10 hours'*. [1]

It was also recorded, that apart from the resident engineer and his assistant, the number of men involved with the project had been 64. On the construction side this amounted to: *'1 clerk; 1 storeman; 1 foreman mason; 22 masons; 6 carpenters; 6 blacksmiths; 2 miners; 6 labourers and 1 millwright'*. [1]

For the steam tug and the schooner: *'there was the Master for each vessel; 2 mates; 2 engineers and 2 firemen for the tug and 14 seamen'*. [1]

Shipwrecks Reduced

By 1872 the value of the Wolf Rock light had warranted the expense. It now provided a distinct navigational reference for this treacherous stretch of water between the Longships Reef and itself. Furthermore, even with the substantial rise in sea trade, the numbers of vessels being lost around Land's End decreased.

Yet with all the favourable publicity in local and national newspapers, Trinity House was subjected to numerous negative criticisms from people who stated that the light should have been established 50 years before. Other comments came from seemingly prominent shipowners, who remarked that the numbers of ships lost would have dropped anyway. The reason being that the rise in ships under steam power had brought about a decline in those using sails. This in turn had allowed the vessels to run straighter and more controllable courses. [4]

All of the various comments and criticisms were answered by a Captain Bartholomew Isaacs, in a letter printed in the Cornwall Gazette. He wrote: *'While others argue the virtues for the light and many more the reverse, no matter how a ship is powered or sailed, if an obstacle is unmarked the chances of collision increases'*.

A Companion Light

Following the successful completion of the Wolf Rock lighthouse, Michael Beazeley was appointed the resident engineer for a new tower to be erected on the Longships Reef. It was intended by Trinity House, for the projects designer William Douglass to supervise the work. However another contract being covered by him made this impossible. [5]

By 1873 the new 117ft (35.66m) high granite tower on the Longships Rock was completed. The Wolf Rock tower now had a prominent companion, and between them they provided one of the best lit shipping lanes around the British Isles.

These two lights also complemented each other during foggy conditions. If the keepers in the lighthouses could not see the adjacent light, they would turn their lamps up to full power and bring into operation their fog warning systems.

Longships lighthouse.
With kind permission of Dave Wilkinson

Costly Wicks

One major expense in lighthouses during the middle of the Victorian era, was the cost of purchasing the wicks for the lamps. Wolf Rock was no exception, yet the number of replacement wicks became one of the most expensive items for this lighthouse.

In 1880 this problem was resolved by the introduction of the constant level lamp. Prior to this time, these burners were basic capillary units which the keepers filled before each night shift. Once in operation the level of the oil dropped, which then caused the upper portion of the wicks to be burnt and charred. Because of the possible dangers, always present when refuelling the hot lamps during the night, these multi-wicks had to be replaced with costly regularity.

James Nicholas Douglass was instrumental in providing an answer to this problem. Wilkins & Son Ltd. also produced its own system. Initially the Wilkins version incorporated a secondary oil tank, hung to one side of the lamp. By means of a gravity drop-feed, the main reservoir was kept at its optimum level. However the Douglass design utilised a system of pressurised paraffin. He devised this equipment which was manufactured by Chance Brothers. Special oil tanks were constructed of zinc-plated iron and sited in the oil rooms, after removing the old wooden tanks. Hand pumps then forced air into these containers, which in turn lifted the pressurised mineral oil through a

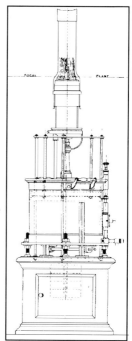

Chance Brothers constant level lamp, similar to the Douglass design. Kind permission of Kenneth Sutton-Jones

29

small-bore pipeline to the lamps. The flow of the fuel was then controlled by a simple weighted ball-cock in the lamp, which equalised the level of the paraffin. The result of this system effectively halved the number of wicks being used and it also reduced the consumption of oil, but not to any great degree. There were other advantages with the Douglass system, with one dispensing the need for the keepers to weigh the remaining oil in the lamps after each night shift. Fitted on the feed line from the oil room was a small flow meter. This unit provided the keepers with an accurate reading of the paraffin used.

Another aspect with the Douglass method also took away the need to filter the remaining paraffin after every shift. Normally this was done to remove any particles of charred wick that may have contaminated the oil. With the addition of a secondary filter put into the lamps, this problem was virtually eliminated. [5]

Exploding Fog Rockets

With more vessels becoming steam powered, the use of fog bells on lighthouses proved to be virtually useless. In most cases they could not be heard above the noise of a steamer's idling engines, and when the ship was fully under way, nothing could be heard at all.

After several close disasters with vessels nearly hitting the Wolf Rock during fog,

Sir Thomas Matthews
With kind permission of Trinity House

Trinity House supplied the station with exploding rockets during the summer of 1889. Initially it was intended to fit a fog gun, but with one already in use on the Longships just eight miles away, Trinity House believed this might be confusing for shipping.

Incandescent Oil Burner – Reed Horn

Although ships were still being lost near the Wolf Rock, these incidents only occurred during exceptional weather conditions. However Trinity House began to receive several complaints, that the services provided by the Wolf Rock station were not congenial to the needs of present day requirements for shipping.

With most vessels making faster and straighter courses, their Masters and Shipowners demanded brighter lights which could be seen from greater distances. The answer to this problem came in 1901, with the invention of a retired gas board engineer, Arthur Kitson, which became known as the incandescent oil burner.

Sir Thomas Matthews, the Corporation's Engineer-in-Chief, implemented a modernisation programme for the Wolf Rock lighthouse in 1904. This upgrading work included the removal of the Douglass multi-wick lamps, and the introduction of the Matthews incandescent oil burner, devised from the Kitson invention. This system utilised the Douglass pressurised paraffin which was fed through a small vaporiser in a retort below a silk mantle. A methylated spirit lamp was placed under the retort, which heated the vapour to a

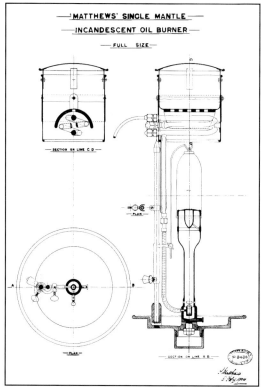

Single mantle incandescent oil burner.
With kind permission of Trinity House

white gas. When this occurred, the gas was ignited above the mantle. Not only did this kind of light source reduce the oil consumption by half, but it effectively trebled the intensity normally associated with multi-wick burners.

The existing fog rockets were stored away in the tower and a new reed horn fitted. Then a small coke and coal burning boiler was installed, producing steam for a small steam engine to power up the air compressor. The air receivers, which supplied the power for the reed horn, were sited in the lantern room. When in service, this fog horn provided a 4 second blast every 30 seconds. Its audible range was considered to be about 6 nautical miles. [7]

At this time a new system of distress flares was provided for the Wolf Rock. In cases of shipping problems, the keepers would send up a rocket that provided a burst of red stars, followed by a sharp explosion. The reply from the mainland would be a flag or an explosion during daytime. However when this happened during the night, the reply would be an exploding rocket emitting white stars.

It had been considered by Trinity House that the Wolf Rock should be painted to with a suitable livery, so that the tower provided a prominent daytime beacon for shipping. But later it was decided to leave the lighthouse in its present state of the grey granite and black lantern.

Wolf Rock at War — 1914–18

Six months before the official announcement of the First World War, the British Admiralty ordered that many of the lighthouses around the British Isles should be set up as observation posts. Trinity House complained about this arrangement because its lighthouses were for humanitarian reasons and not objects of war, but the instruction was backed by the Government. The politicians reminded the Corporation about the terms of its Charter, which insisted that Trinity House was obliged to provide men at sea during a time of war. Although this was considered to mean *'with ships'* in its original context, the Elder Brethren accepted the instruction. Yet they refused to allow their lighthouses to be armed.

Between 1914-18 the keepers on the Wolf Rock were ordered to extinguish the lights. They were only allowed to re-light them at half power for the passing of Allied convoys. At times these convoys stretched for miles as they made their way down the St. George's and Bristol Channels, with German U-boats picking off these slow moving and unarmed vessels in tragic numbers. The stretch of water between the Longships and the Wolf Rock became one of the favourite hunting grounds for these submarines. They were intent on ensuring that these coal carrying ships were not able to supply the hungry boilers of the British warships. Even after running the gauntlet near Land's End, these easy targets were subjected to further attacks as they made their way up the English Channel. During these times the keepers in both the Longships and Wolf Rock lighthouse, kept records of the devastation caused by these seemingly unstoppable submerged assassins.

By the end of the First World War the waters around Land's End were littered with twisted shipwrecks, which had become the deep watery graves for numerous mariners. [4]

A Different Kind Of Enemy — 1939–45

Shortly before the start of the Second World War, the Wolf Rock lighthouse had its first radio telephone installed. Although battery operated, this wall mounted phone finally provided a welcome link to the outside world. To operate this unit, a handle was first turned to obtain a link with the mainland. When a call was received, the two small bells on its oak board would ring. The introduction of this telephone would assist the keepers during their time as observers.

Many lives were saved because of the keepers' actions in contacting the rescue services, when a ship had been attacked or if any enemy shipping was sighted. More importantly they were able to give early warning of the new menace of this war, and that was from the Luftwaffe. However, the keepers on the Wolf Rock must have lived in fear each night, especially when considering that German aircraft gunners regularly used this lighthouse for target practise. On several occasions the lantern was shot at, with resulting bullet-holes through the roof and the catadioptric apparatus. The only place the keepers could hide was near the base of the tower, where the thickness of the walls protected them.

Yet the perilous waters near the Longships and Wolf Rock proved to be far too dangerous for the U–boats, which tried to hide close to these stations and out of range of the sonar detectors on board the British warships. Losses for German shipping around the Wolf Rock were mostly submarines. On the 18th December 1944, U-1209 was patrolling around Land's End and ran into the Wolf Rock. Nearly all its crew perished, with the survivors being picked up by a British warship following a message received from the keepers in the lighthouse. [4]

By the end of the Second World War, the sea around the Wolf Rock had become a tragic graveyard for numerous German and Allied vessels. The loss of lives was tragic. Amongst those submarines sunk by British aircraft or warships were the U-683, U-480 and the U-1199. In each case it was recorded, that of their crews had been lost. [4]

When considering the reasons behind these tragic losses during the Second World War, it proves that no-one won the battle. In reality war has no friends, only allies or enemies. But the greatest tragedy is that of the real losers, who are those people that had no means of defence. *'If politicians put as much effort into preventing a war, as they do in celebrating its end, the World would be a safer place to live in'*. [13]

Repairs to Lighthouses – Sir John Bowen

By the time the War was over, Sir John Bowen had been appointed the Engineer in Chief for Trinity House, on the retirement of Sir Thomas Matthews. One of his main instructions from the Corporation was to restore the navigational lights around England, the Channel Islands and Wales, into a fully operational status.

At the Longstone station, off the Northumbrian coast, the major portion of the former

Sir John Bowen
With kind permision of Trinity House

Grace Darling lighthouse had to be rebuilt. Yet the devastating bombing by the Luftwaffe had left her previous bedroom completely intact. [7]

Although the main part of the St. Catherine's station, on the Isle of Wight, was unharmed, the engine room had to be rebuilt. This building held a sad reminder for the families of three keepers who had died following a direct hit from a German bomb.

Sir John Bowen organised the Trinity House repair crews, who concentrated on those stations which had suffered disabilitating damage. The Wolf Rock was not considered to be one of these lighthouses, for there was surprisingly little damage, even after the numerous attacks by the Luftwaffe. The necessary repairs were carried out in 1947. Even then this work was only temporary, with just the copper sheeting renewed to its conical roof, and several full and half diamond panes of glass replaced in its helical lantern. Work to repair the damaged optical apparatus was confined to renewing just those prisms that were considered to be most important. When Chance Brothers was asked to price for a new optic, the cost was found to be exceptionally high. Arrangements were then made by Sir John Bowen for upgrading the Wolf Rock lighthouse a few years later.

During these minor repairs, Trinity House had a new valve-operated radio-telephone installed, which was manufactured by Pye Electronics. This particular 'Pye Hamble' unit was one of the first of its kind to be put into an offshore lighthouse. [7]

Stormbound With No Relief

During the latter part of November 1947, the west coasts of England and Ireland were subject to one of the most devastating and prolonged periods of storm and gales. At times the wind reached near hurricane force, as it battered the lonely rock-based lighthouses. For nearly eight weeks the keepers in the Fastnet lighthouse had been overdue for their relief, and by January 1948 the provisions were almost gone and their tobacco all used up.

Along the west coast of England such stations as the Eddystone, Longships, Wolf and Bishop Rock began to feel the tremendous power of these storms during the beginning of January 1948. At this time the keepers on the Wolf Rock were about 22 days overdue for their relief, and their provisions were down to just four days supply. Britain's youngest keeper at this time, 20 year old Stanley MacClary, managed to power up the faulty radio at the Wolf Rock, and to relay a message to Captain Joseph Reseigh, the Master of the SCILLONIAN. As the steamer passed the lighthouse, he asked the Captain if he could signal the Trinity House depot at Penzance and inform, the Superintendent Captain C. H. White, that they were desperately short of provisions. The response, reported by a correspondent for the News Chronicle in Cornwall, stated that an official Trinity House source remarked *'They must have been eating their heads off if they've got through their iron rations.'*

Captain White, at the Penzance Depot, responded without delay to the report from the Master of the SCILLONIAN, and got the necessary supplies loaded on board the Trinity House tender TRITON. Within hours this vessel was underway, towards the stricken keepers on the Wolf Rock. The intention was to send the provisions in waterproof containers, slung from a rope between the TRITON and the landing stage. But as the TRITON circled the Rock, the heavy sea and spray was ranging to nearly halfway up to the tower, which forced the attempt to be aborted. Although messages were relayed by morse lamps between the Tender and the keepers, there was nothing anyone could do to reach the Rock.

At the beginning of February 1948, Trinity House, along with the Admiralty, began to make preparations for using a helicopter to relieve the keepers stranded on the Wolf Rock. A Westland Sikorsky S51 stood by at the Culdrose Naval Air Station near the Lizard Point, waiting for the weather to be favourable for making the dangerous attempt. On the 5th February the skilful flying of the helicopter pilot allowed the desperately needed supplies to be lowered onto the gallery of the Wolf Rock tower. At this time the wind was still extremely high, with the spray from the heavy seas reaching halfway up towards the lantern. It was a further 10 days before the keepers were finally taken off the Wolf Rock, and back to the Penzance Depot.

Wolf Rock lighthouse during the modernisation. With kind permission of Trinity House

New Lens and Electrification

The delayed modernisation programme began in 1955, and for this important work Trinity House stationed two lightvessels close to the Wolf Rock. Notifications about the pending work had been posted in all the relative ports around the British Isles and Ireland, while overseas ports were informed in the normal fashion via the International Maritime Agency.

The main part of this contract was the electrification of the lighthouse, with this work carried out by G.E.C. Electrics Ltd., in conjunction with Chance Brothers. The existing fog horn and optic were also removed.

The new optical assembly was a 4th order catadioptric apparatus, plus its electri-

*Chance Brothers 4th. order catadioptric apparatus
and new clockwork mechanism on Wolf Rock.
With kind permission of Gerry Douglas-Sherwood*

cally driven revolving pedestal base. Although the original Wilkins & Son clockwork mechanism was removed, a new Chance Brothers clockwork was installed in its place. This unit was specially designed to allow for any of the bearings or cogs to be removed with the whole mechanism still in situ. Former systems required the dismantling of the complete assembly before any replacement parts could be fitted.

The new 4th order optical apparatus was designed by Kenneth Sutton-Jones, who ensured that the specifications of the red and white intensity remained equal. He also supervised the actual setting of the optic on the Wolf Rock. However, when this apparatus was sited in the centre of the lantern room, its size looked completely out of character when compared to the existing majestic lantern.

A 1kW tungsten filament lamp, with an automatic two position changer was installed as the new light source for the optic. This assembly was designed and manufactured by Chance Brothers, soon to became Stone & Chance. The principle behind this changer was based upon the continual flow of electricity through the completed circuit. If the bulb failed, this unit rotated and brought into service the second lamp. A further backup-system was provided by a battery powered 50volt – 500watt lamp, that automatically came into operation if there was a total mains failure. It allowed the lamp to remain operational for up to 72 hours of active service. If these electrical systems failed, either through loss of battery power, or because service technicians could not get to the lighthouse due to bad weather conditions, the keepers could remove the lamp assembly and install a Douglass multi-wick oil burner. [7]

Electrical Supply

Two Crompton Parkinson 2.5kW–100V d.c. generator sets were installed in the redundant coal store, and driven by Ruston-Hornsby type 2 Y.B., 5hp radiator cooled diesel engines. A third generator set, driven by a 10hp engine, provided a power of 5.5kW/100V d.c.

The oil room was converted, with two large diesel storage tanks installed, while two of the existing paraffin containers were retained for fuelling the emergency Douglass oil burner.

Two small pressurised oil tanks were now fitted in the service room, linked with a small-bore copper feed pipe to the pedestal base of the optic in the lantern room. Even this pedestal base had a backup system. In the event of electrical failure or the wire for weight drive breaking and no replacement available, the keepers had to revolve the optic by a small handle. With the use of a stopwatch and timing marks on the pedestal base, the keepers ensured that the assigned characteristic, of the now hand-driven apparatus, remained true.

When the modernisation programme was completed in October 1955, the intensity of the Wolf Rock light was recorded at 350,000 candle power, with a visible range of about 16 nautical miles. [7]

Electrical Supply. With kind permission of Gerry Douglas-Sherwood

37

Diaphone Fog Warning System

The Wolf Rock lighthouse was one of the last Trinity House stations to be fitted with a diaphone fog unit. This system was similar in principle as a siren, except it used a reciprocating slotted piston inside of a cylinder with matching slots. As the piston was forced upwards by compressed air, a loud melodious note was produced. These units were well known for their characteristic 'grunt' at the end of each cycle of operation. The original steam boiler and air compressor were replaced by a new Lister combination set. The compressed air from this unit was fed into two receivers sited in the lantern room, which in turn powered the diaphone unit on the gallery. Although not recorded as ever being used, was an emergency backup system. This Norwegian pattern fog signal was a portable hand-held device in a large wooden box. The keepers were intended to wind the handle on its side to make it work, but all that could be said about this thing was, that it was 'mind bogglingly useless'. [12]

Chance Brothers diaphone unit.
Showing gas engines and air compressors in
duplicate, with siren at side (around 1910)

When the diaphone fog signal was in operation, it was set to provide a 2.5 second blast every 30 seconds and was recorded as having an audible range of 8 nautical miles. [7]

Tragic Circumstances of the JEANNE GOUGY

At about 05.00 hours on the 3rd November 1962, Cornish Coastguards saw the lights of a large trawler about two miles off shore. On her present heading it appeared the ship would clear Land's End then change course towards Dieppe. Yet for some inexplicable reason this did not occur, which placed the vessel in direct line with the Wolf Rock. Coastguards and the keepers at both the Longships and the Wolf Rock fired off warning flares, which they believed had been noticed. However the trawler made a sudden change of course, but never acknowledged the flares. This time she was heading directly towards the Cornish coast, with the weather turning rough and heavy swells.

Further flares were sent up, but again they went unanswered. Within half an hour, red star flares were sighted above the cliffs near the Land's End Hotel. Rescue services raced to the scene to find the 250 ton trawler JEANNE GOUGY on the rocks near Gamper Bay. It was also noticed that there was a very strong smell of diesel that filling the air near the wrecked ship.

Coastguards sent up parachute flares which revealed a group of men, huddled together near the bridge of the trawler. Rocket powered safety lines were fired on to the stricken vessel, but as a crewman tried to catch one, a huge wave swept him overboard. Suddenly a mountainous wave threw the trawler on her side and under a tangle of nets and debris. All of the onlookers felt helpless and believed she had become a dead ship, with the loss of everyone on board.

At about 09.30 hours the Sennen lifeboat picked up the body of the first seaman who had been washed overboard, and about half an hour later a helicopter from RAF Chivenor had located another.

It was decided by the Coastguards and other rescue services, that it was extremely doubtful that anyone had survived. At just after 10.00 hours, the helicopter was instructed to carry out one last search before returning to base. With this done, the helicopter left the scene, but 10 minutes later a woman amongst the onlookers shouted, that she had seen a hand waving from the wheelhouse. As the rescue services were recalled to the scene, a huge wave smashed away part of the wheelhouse to reveal four crewmen, who now climbed out on to the shattered decking.

Just as the helicopter was about to land at RAF Chivenor, the pilot was ordered to return. On its arrival it hovered over the wrecked JEANNE GOUGY while lines were thrown to the surviving crewmen by the Coastguards. Within 20 minutes the battered men were hoisted to safety, but there was still an injured man inside the shattered wheelhouse. In atrocious conditions Flight Sergeant Eric Smith talked the pilot of the helicopter into allowing him to be lowered, to try and rescue the stricken seaman. After much turbulence and manoeuvring of the helicopter, he was able to put a sling around the seaman and hoist him to the safety of the cliffs above. Although Flt. Sgt. Smith was told it was extremely unlikely that anyone else could have survived, he insisted on being lowered back on to the trawler for a closer look. As he swung to the rear of the battered bridge, he was surprised to find a small terrified and sodden boy. Even though he was battered against the bridge by the strong winds and the sea, he managed to rescue the boy and lift him to safety.

Not satisfied with leaving the incident at that stage he insisted on going back once more, to see if there were any more people to be found. Only after the pilot was forced to give him a direct order to return to the helicopter, did Flt. Sgt Smith relent.

In the Royal Cornwall Gazette the same day, it was reported that the death-toll for the JEANNE GOUGY was 10 men and her captain. No reason has ever been provided as to why this tragedy occurred, the knowledge sadly died with her captain. The Board of Trade enquiry left the reasons as an *open verdict* and refused to make any comment whether the captain was at fault, because he was not there to defend himself.

Flight Sergeant Smith was later awarded the George Medal for his actions. [8]

It would seem that this area of the Cornish coast had already seen enough evidence of the treacherous forces of the sea. Also that vessels around this stretch of water would be only too aware of the dangers. Yet less than 18 months after the JEANNE GOUGY disaster, another trawler ran aground just 200 yards (183m) from where she was wrecked.

In atrocious weather conditions on the 24th March 1964, the 90 ton VICTORIE ROGER was forced aground. On this occasion all of her crew were saved by the Sennen Lifeboat, whose men refused to leave until all the survivors were on board. During the operation the coxswain positioned his Lifeboat against the rocks, so his crew could rescue an injured seaman. As the Lifeboat pulled away from the scene, a huge wave rolled the VICTORIE ROGER over on her side, and within minutes she sank. [4]

Strange Occurrence of the Missing Keeper

A mystery still surrounds the tragic loss of a keeper on the Wolf Rock lighthouse. On the 18th December 1969, this keeper was last seen fishing from the winch room. The safety barrier was set in its correct position, which was designed to prevent anyone from falling, even if he were standing up. His disappearance has never been explained, though various theories have been put forward. Although a full search of the area was made by the Lifeboat and a Trinity House helicopter, his body was never found. An 'open verdict' was recorded by the Coroner.

First Rock Based Lighthouse with a Helipad

On the 3rd November 1973, the Wolf Rock lighthouse became the first rock-based tower to have a helipad erected above its lantern. This event received world-wide acclaim and publicity, and from this successful project, Trinity House installed helipads on most of its offshore lighthouses. The obvious advantage of a helicopter was for the resulting ease in relieving the keepers, and the dropping of necessary supplies. From now on, it was only on very rare occasions that the weather prevented a landing. Yet the pilot would need to remain with his helicopter, with the propellers still turning, in case the high winds blew the aircraft off the helipad. Instead of the keepers being stranded for weeks at a time, they could be lifted from their desolate locations in a matter of hours.

To ensure the helipad was fully functional and swiftly assembled onto the

Helicopter on Wolf Rock helipad at Blackwall.
With kind permission of Trinity House

Wolf Rock lantern, it was first erected at the Blackwall experimental station, next to the River Lee, near the Thames. Various problems were encountered by the technicians, who actually acted out the erecting programme, to duplicate the same working conditions they would face out on the Wolf Rock.

Nothing was left to chance, with many modifications made, to ensure that the final structure would actually fit together. Once this had been done, it was dismantled and put into labelled crates and sent to Penzance in a kit form. However, it can be proved by the photo in this publication, that the date given for the first helicopter landing on the Wolf Rock helipad is incorrect. This event actually occured at Blackwall, on the 19th March 1973.

Within a few years the helicopter would begin the demise of the lighthouse keeper. Not only did it provide a safe and regular means to relieve them, but it brought Trinity House

Wolf Rock helipad, trap door and ladder to gallery. With kind permission of Gerry Douglas-Sherwood

engineers and numerous pieces of equipment, which would bring about the automation of the station. During this time advanced lighthouse technology, and the means to control it without the manual task, sounded like a death bell for the keepers. [10]

Final Days of the Keepers - Automation

On the 3rd June 1987, the last of the traditional keepers left the Wolf Rock lighthouse for the final time. Their expected airlift by helicopter was a day late, due to foggy conditions around the station.

These keepers were Ian Patterson P.K., who had served with Trinity House for 26 years. Before joining the lighthouse service, he had spent 14 years with the United States Navy and on leaving entered the British merchant navy. His companions on the Wolf Rock were David Nollan A.K. and Dave Robbins A.K. Although officially the last keepers, their relieving crew should not be forgotten. They included Tony Homewood, temporary P.K., George Carthew A.K. and Clive Harry A.K.

When the helicopter finally arrived to take off the keepers, it also brought out a small team of Trinity House engineers, who would continue with the automation programme and tend the light etc., until the official hand-over to the Operations Directorate of the Corporation, on the 18th July 1988.

Using control systems devised during the 1970's, similar to those used in space exploration, the Wolf is now monitored by telemetry link from the Regional Operations Centre at Harwich. Prior to the automation being completed, the red sector light was discontinued. Its main light was increased to a 1.5 kW light source, which produced an intensity through the optic of about 378,000 candle power. It now gives out a white flash every 15 seconds, with a recorded distance of 23 nautical miles. [11]

During the times when the keepers were in attendance on the Wolf Rock, their feelings about this particular station were varied. Most of them have openly commented about the effect of the storms and high seas, which pounded this isolated granite tower. At times anything in the kitchen which was not securely put away would be shaken off the tables and cupboards, smashed on the floor. Spray regularly cascaded over the lantern, which distorted the beams of light. Condensation inside of the tower became a regular problem, with mopping-up of the water being one of the routine chores. With the station now automated, who will clean up the mess?

Keepers at Wolf Rock entrance with Christmas tree.
With kind permisson of Trinity House

When compared to other rock-based stations around England, Ireland, Scotland and Wales, its claustrophobic and confined quarters were very similar to the Bell Rock, off the Scottish coast. At both of these stations, many keepers felt they were serving a prison sentence every time they covered their tours of duty. It is therefore clear, that to endure the conditions in these particular lighthouses, it took a very special breed of keeper.

Today, the lonely sentinel of the Wolf Rock lighthouse stands proudly off the Cornish coast. It represents an important monument for the expertise of its designer, and the skills of the men who built her. Even after nearly 130 years of treacherous weather conditions and mountainous seas, she continues her important service as a navigation aid for the mariner.

Wolf Rock lighthouse in 1980. With kind permission of Trinity House

REFERENCE SOURCES

1. Douglass, J. N., 'The Wolf Rock Lighthouse',
   Minutes Of The Proceedings Of The Institution Of Civil Engineers,
   Vol. 30. No. 268, 1-28, (1870)
2. Trinity House Records (August 1791) - Guildhall Library London
3. Trinity House Records (April 1797) - Guildhall Library London
4. Noall, C., 'Cornish Lights And Shipwrecks'
   Published By D. Bradford Ltd., Truro, Cornwall (1968)
5. Williams, T., 'Life Of Sir James Nicholas Douglass' (1900) 'Private Edition'
6. Williams, T., 'Life Of William Douglass' (1923) 'Private Edition'
7. Trinity House Engineering Records, (18th June 1955 and 20th November 1955)
8. Royal Cornwall Gazette (5th November, 1962)
9. Trinity House Records (18th December, 1969)
   Guildhall Library, London.
10. Trinity House Engineering Records (1973) London.
11. Trinity House Records, Tower Hill, London (1995)
12. Records Of The Association Of Lighthouse Keepers (1996)
13. Ted Jones, Son of former St. Catherine's keeper (1997)

ACKNOWLEDGEMENTS FROM THE AUTHOR

A special 'thank you' is given to all those people and organisations who have so 'willingly' assisted in ensuring that the details portrayed in this publication were 'factual'. These include Ian Beevis, Karl Spitzer and Hans Spitzer, Gerry Douglas-Sherwood (archivist for the ALK), Jane Wilson for Trinity House, Kenneth Sutton Jones and Pharos Marine, with last but not least David Wilkinson of the Royal Lifeboat Enthusiasts Association, who had helped with many details relating to the various ship wrecks.

Mention must also made about the 'anonymous' Trinity House photographers and draught 'persons', who have provided a pictorial record that allows a special insight into this lighthouse story. Many lunch-breaks were disturbed during my research, so my special thanks to Frank Celanco and Johns Sims of the Engineering Directorate, for their invaluable assistance.

A particular 'thank you' is given to Frank Gibson and his family, for providing so many exceptional photos for use in this publication. Other pictures have come from numerous keepers, such as Reg Simon, Gerry Douglas-Sherwood and Barry Hawkins, who has given an insight in other publications of his exceptional talents as an artist.

Many documents were researched with a great deal of information being supplied by the Cornish Studies Library in Redruth, Cornwall. Without a doubt the assistance of the very friendly and helpful staff at this library is 'heart warming' to any 'probing' author.

The help from the Institution of Civil Engineers in London and the archivists of the Public Record Office, the Guildhall Library and the Truro Record Office is particularly acknowledged.

Like all jig-saw puzzles, it can not be considered finished until every piece is in place. To put anyone in any particular order of priority is impossible, because without all the pieces this 'puzzle' would not have been completed.

THANK YOU ALL

Martin Boyle

ASSOCIATION OF LIGHTHOUSE KEEPERS
The Secretary · 2 Queen's Cottages · Queen's Road · Lydd · Kent · TN29 9ND

Formed in 1988 by a group of serving and retired keepers. Its aim to forge links with other associations and societies throughout the World. The Association has an extensive archive and aims to establish an International Museum and study centre. Open to membership for all enthusiasts.

TRINITY HOUSE · National Lighthouse Museum
Wharf Road · Penzance · Cornwall · TR18 4BN · Tel. (+44) (01736) 360077

A must for every enthusiast and anyone interested in the history of maritime safety.

SCOTLAND'S LIGHTHOUSE MUSEUM
Kinnaird Head · Fraserburg · Aberdeenshire Scotland · AB43 9DU
Tel. (+44) (01346) 511022 · Fax (+44) (01346) 511033

A very comprehensive collection of lighthouse artifacts from across Scotland and the Isles. The purpose built Museum sits across the headland from Kinnaird Head lighthouse. A visit to the Museum also includes a guided tour to the top of the lighthouse, which was one of four, originally established by the Commissioners of the Northern Lights around 1785. Very helpful staff, who are extremely proud of the Northern Lighthouse Board Heritage. The Museum also has an extensive collection of photographs, a library, study centre and archives. Well worth the visit.

LEADING LIGHTS MAGAZINE
Peter Williams Associates · c/o Haven Lightship · Milford Marina · Milford Haven · SA73 3AF
Tel (+44) (01646) 698055/698825

Now established as the International Lighthouse Journal. Numerous contributions and articles by lighthouse enthusiasts from all over the World. Also very much involved with the preservation of former lightvessels. Peter Williams Associates manage the Haven Lightship moored in Milford Marina, Milford Haven, where it is possible to stay overnight or for holiday.

ANDREW BESELEY
Photographer & Photographic Library
2 Reawla Lane · Reawla · Nr. Hayle · Cornwall · TR27 5HQ · Tel. (+44) (01736) 850086

This professional photographer has even hung from the side of a helicopter in rather bad weather to obtain the right shot. His library is well worth visit.

STICHTING HISTORIE DER KUSTVERLICHTING
Kemphaanstraat 42 · 1701 WS · Den Helder · Netherlands

The aims of the foundation are collecting and maintaining lighthouse and lightship related material. They are rebuilding the famous lightvessel TEXEL to its manned status, and maintain historical equipment in the lighthouses of Scheveningen and Hook of Holland. Visitors, volunteers and donations are welcome.

LIGHTHOUSE DIGEST

P.O. Box 1690 · Wells · Maine 04090 · USA
Tel. (+1) 207 - 646 - 0515 · Fax (+1) 207 - 646 - 0516

The world's only monthly (full colour) lighthouse magazine, with a wide range of articles covering past and presence of American and international lighthouses. Always up-to-date with the monthly Calendar of Events.

U.S. LIGHTHOUSE SOCIETY

c/o Wayne Wheeler · 244 Kearny Street · 5th Floor
San Francisco · CA 94108 · USA · Tel. (+1) 415 - 362 - 7255 · Fax (+1) 415 - 362 - 7464

America's most successful Lighthouse Society was founded in 1984 and has now over 10,000 members. Their official quarterly publication, 'THE KEEPER'S LOG', is an excellent high-gloss magazine, which paints a vivid picture of the history of American lighthouses.

INTERNATIONAL ASSOCIATION OF LIGHTHOUSE AUTHORITIES (IALA)

c/o Paul Ridgeway · 3 The Green · Ketton · Stamford · Lincolnshire · PE9 3RA
Tel. (+44) (01780) 721628 · Fax (+44) (01780) 721980

Specialist contact for information on past and current policies of the members of all the Lighthouse Corporations and Authorities around the World. Any data needed by the enthusiast or mariner relating to future use of lighthouses or other maritime aids can be obtained from IALA. Its journal 'BULLETIN' is produced every four month.

 German Lighthouse Enthusiasts Magazine

C/o Klaus Kern · Pestalozzistrasse 28 · D–65428 Rüsselsheim · Germany · Tel. (+49) (06142) 81607

News of lighthouses, lightships and other seamarks. Plus book reviews, postage stamps and post-cards. Numerous up-to-date news items about navigational aids and the preservation of lighthouses and lightships from all over the world. This splendid magazine is produced every four months.

SWEDEN'S LIGHTHOUSE SOCIETY

c/o Esbjörn Hillberg · HUS 154 · S–43082 Donsö · Sweden
Tel. (+46) (0) 31–972148 · Fax (+46) (0) 31–970623

Founded October 1996 by E. Hillberg of Donsö. Constantly growing membership. All enquiries welcome.

THE TREVITHICK TRUST

Chygarth · 5 Beacon Terrace · Camborne · Cornwall · TR14 7BU
Telephone/Fax 01209 612142

THE
TREVITHICK
TRUST

The objective of the Trust is to identify, preserve, protect, manage, and interpret for the benefit of the people of Cornwall and for the public at large throughout the world of the historical, architectural and engineering heritage may exist, in the form of buildings, artifacts, documents, records and land associated with Cornish mining and engineering, and related industries and activities, including the Pendeen lighthouse.

FRANK E. GIBSON
St Mary's Island · Isles of Scilly · Cornwall · TR21 0QJ · Tel. (+44) (01720) 422654
*Photographer of numerous Cornish Lights and a very modest man
with regards to his exceptional talents.*

MARITIME HERITAGE TOURS LIMITED
Tour Operator Specialising in Maritime Attractions Past & Present

Seaways House · 26 Grange Avenue · Ryde · Isle of Wight · UK · PO33 3LS
Tel. (+44) 01983 562484 · Fax (+44) 01983 563105 · e-mail: m_walter@martours.demon.co.uk

*Maritime Heritage Tours have put together a special selection of tours, accompanied by experienced
couriers, which will encompass lighthouses and other maritime venues around the U.K. and abroad.
Ask for special rates for members of our B&T Book- or Pen Pal Club, the ALK and other Lighthouse
and Maritime Organisations.*

LIFEBOAT ENTHUSIASTS SOCIETY
c/o John G. Francis · 'Cadleigh' · 13 West Way · Petts Wood
Orpington · Kent · BR5 1LN

*This Society was founded in 1964. Today it has a membership of 800,
which is spread throughout the U.K. and overseas. A newsletter, which is
published three times a year, contains technical development, lifeboat
services, station details, lifeboat movements, historical features, modelling, with member photographs, stories and postcards etc. The is also the official RNLI publication 'THE LIFEBOAT JOUR-
NAL' which every member receives quarterly. Local research groups have also been formed which
cover the North East, North West, East and South East coasts. For further details about the membership write to the above address. Please enclose a stamped addressed envelope.*

HANS-GÜNTER SPITZER
c/o B&T Publications · 10 Orchard Way · Highfield Southampton
SO17 1RD · U.K.

Typesetting · Logos · Drawings: »The Spitzer Collection«

Also available in this series are the following publications:

NEEDLES POINT

PORTLAND BILL

LIGHTHOUSES — FOUR COUNTRIES – ONE AIM

LIGHTHOUSES — TO LIGHT THEIR WAY

EDDYSTONE

BISHOP ROCK

LONGSHIPS

SKERRIES ROCK

47

To obtain a free list of 'LIGHTHOUSES OF ENGLAND AND WALES' booklets and the details of our 'NO OBLIGATION TO BUY' bookclub, send a S.A.E. to B&T PUBLICATIONS, 10 Orchard Way, Highfield, Southampton, S017 1RD, U.K.

To accompany this collection of 'LIGHTHOUSES OF ENGLAND AND WALES', the author has compiled two special publications. The first booklet is titled: 'LIGHT-HOUSES: FOUR COUNTRIES, ONE AIM' and gives an easy to read insight into the Corporation of Trinity House, the Commissioners of Irish Lights, the Commissioners of Northern Lights, Private Lighthouse owners, Royal Letter-Patents and the services which are provided today. This booklet also gives an account of the designers and builders of the lighthouses around the coasts of the British Isles.

The second publication provided a detailed account of the various light sources, fuels, reflectors and optical apparatus, lanterns and fog warning sytems and an insight to those designers and manufacturers who supplied these items. Titled: 'LIGHT-HOUSES: TO LIGHT THEIR WAY', this booklet had been produced with many archive photos and pictorials which have been provided by the various Lighthouse Authorities and by the author of 'PHAROS: THE LIGHTHOUSE YESTERDAY, TODAY AND TOMORROW', Kenneth Sutton-Jones. This author has also assisted in a major way, by ensuring that the relative technical details are correct. His help has been greatly appreciated by the author. Each of these booklets can be obtained from bookshops or direct from the publisher, (POST FREE IN UK).

Also available from B&T PUBLICATIONS:

Database of the Lighthouses of Great Britain and Ireland. Full colour Windows® (3.1, 3.11 and 95) software. References and locations for over 350 lighthouses. Details of characteristic, fog signals, lat/long, type of tower, date established, history and sources of information. Modify the database to suit your own needs. Comprehensive Search and Help functions. Suitable for PCs 386 and above with 4Mb RAM and VGA screen. Requires 2MB hard disk space and 3.5" floppy drive. Not suitable for Apple-Mac.

»THE SPITZER COLLECTION« – numerous drawings of lighthouses, lightvessels, lanterns and optics by H.-G. Spitzer (see example of Wolf Rock on page 23), printed on parchment paper, size A4.

Why not join the PHAROS PEN PAL CLUB?
Details from the Secretary:
Ian Beevis · 13 Chyngton Way · Seaford · East Sussex · BN25 4JB · U.K.